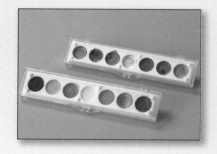

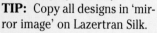

Lazertran Silk

Many techniques have been developed for transferring images onto polymer clay. Each has unique results. Lazertran Silk transfer paper is used for all of the projects in this book. It was chosen for its easy transfer technique and the high quality of the image that is transferred onto unbaked polymer clay.

TIP: Copy all designs in 'mirror image' on Lazertran Silk.

Frames

Many projects in this book use small brass frames in the design. These are generally raw brass which should be washed, dried and sealed with a clear matte acrylic spray before using to retard tarnishing over time. These frames can be used as is or treated with paint or patinas.

Metallic Rub-Ons

These projects use Metallic Rub-Ons because they can be applied to polymer clay before baking. The application of Flecto Varathane Diamond Wood Finish after baking gives the clay a unique metallic look.

Finishes

There are a variety of varnishes formulated for use with polymer clay. The projects in this book use Flecto Varathane Diamond Wood Finish (satin), not originally designed for clay.

Flecto Varathane is compatible with clay, user friendly, water soluble, non-toxic and dries clear and flexible.

Create your own mini-masterpieces by transferring the images onto polymer clay.

Mini-masterpieces make fabulous jewelry, beautiful books and wonderful home accessories. You'll treasure every piece.

Selecting Your Images

The images selected as focal points for projects in this book are all mini-masterpieces. They are faces, figures and details from works of art that have, for the most part, been forgotten. Their new lives allow us to appreciate them in a form quite different from the original.

There are several considerations in selecting an image for a mini-masterpiece project. First, it should be copyright free. The best way to insure this is to use your own original artwork. If you choose to use the work of other artists, be sure there are no copyright restrictions. This is a complex issue but, generally, works created before 1923 are now in the public domain.

Wonderful images can be gleaned from 19th century engravings, Victorian advertising, cards, early 1900's postcards, old books and similar sources. Dover publications are also valuable sources of copyright-free images. And don't forget old family photos...yours or other people's.

Another consideration is the suitability of the image for presentation in a small format. Mini-masterpiece images often measure less than 2". Look for images with clear details and strong contrasts. Pick out a single element from a larger picture, such as 1 face in a group, to be the focal point. With a little research and experimentation, you will find images that are perfect for creating your own mini-masterpiece projects.

The 3 pictures to the right illustrate how much the look and style of an image can be changed by selection choices.

Transfer Your Image to Clay

1. Cut out image that has been transferred onto Lazertran Silk transfer paper.

2. Place image face down on clay, burnish with a bone folder.

3. Place clay in a tub of water until the paper detaches.

Transferring
Your Image to Clay

Image Transfer

MATERIALS: Copyright-free images or your own art work • Lazertran Silk transfer paper • White polymer clay • Tissue blade • Bone folder • Small tub of water • Tweezers • Waxed or parchment paper • Paper towel

INSTRUCTIONS:

Have images color copied onto Lazertran Silk transfer paper according to manufacturer's directions. Copies must be made on a toner-based machine, not ink jet. The images should be reversed, or mirror image, if you want the finished piece to look the same as the original. Cut out your image, leaving at least ¼" of White border. Condition White polymer clay, roll out to thickness required. The clay surface should be very smooth, no bubbles or nicks. Trim clay to slightly larger that the image, place on a piece of non-stick paper. Place image face down on clay, rub it gently with your finger. Burnish image firmly with bone folder. Put the clay, image side up, in a small tub of water until the paper floats off the surface of the clay. Remove paper with tweezers, then remove the clay and let it sit for 1 minute. Use a smooth paper towel to remove any remaining moisture. Pat, don't rub. The transferred image may be used immediately or later.

TIP #1: Images transferred onto White clay have the truest colors; however, any light colored clay may be used. Experiment to see what effects can be achieved with Pearl, Ivory or Ecru clay.

TIP #2: Apply chalk with a sponge applicator to add color or to age a Black and White image. Do this before baking.

4. After 1 minute, pat clay gently with a paper towel to remove remaining moisture.

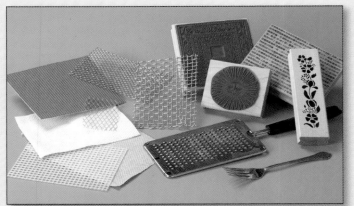

Rubber stamps, plastic texture sheets, fabric and wire mesh, kitchen utensils and wire screen are just a few items that can be used to create interesting textures.

Chrysanthemum Embossed Book

MATERIALS: Image, Chrysanthemum girl • Metal coaster for texture • Black clay • 1¼" Square brass frame • Copper Metallic Rub-On

INSTRUCTIONS: See pages 14-15 Book and Book Cover instructions.

Lady in a Hat Book

MATERIALS: Images, Lady with Hat and French Script • Vintage playing card box for texture • Burnt Umber clay • 1½" and 1¼" Square brass frames • Deep Gold, Blue and Olive Metallic Rub-Ons

INSTRUCTIONS: See pages 14-15 Book and Book Cover instructions.

𝒯exture 𝒨olds
for Book Covers and Other Projects

There are many ways to add texture to polymer clay. Commercially made rubber stamps and plastic texture sheets are available in a variety of designs. Common household items such as kitchen utensils, fabric and wire screen can also be used to create interesting patterns.

All of these can be applied directly to clay, although some may require a release agent such as water, cornstarch or Armor All to prevent sticking. Pressing an object directly into clay produces a negative of the original design.

To duplicate the image exactly, make a mold that can then be used to impress the clay.

1. Roll out a sheet of clay slightly larger than the textured object. This is a good way to use up scraps or leftover colors.

2. Apply a release agent such as cornstarch to textured object.

3. Press object evenly into clay, then carefully remove it without distorting the image. Bake. You can now use this as a mold.

aésites ne vous concer
, je vais vous indiq
acls vous devez vous
ntrez dans une mais
, puis saluez partie
assenez que anand i

Actual project size: 2" x 2"

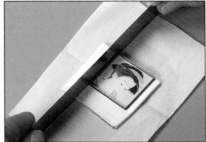

1. Push frame partially into clay, trim edges. Repeat until frame is flush with your work surface.

2. Apply Gold Metallic Rub-On to stamped clay.

3. Lay #5 sheet of clay on the back of framed base, brayer on.

4. Apply Flecto Varathane to base with a bristle brush before gluing the frames into place.

Geisha Pin or Pendant

MATERIALS: Basic Tool Kit • Image, Geisha Head transferred onto #1 White clay (See pages 4-5) • Black clay • Translucent *Liquid Sculpey* (TLS) • *Hero Arts* Chinese Newspaper WordPrint rubber stamp• 1¼" Square brass frame • 2" Square brass frame • Metallic Rub-Ons • Sponge applicator • *Flecto* Varathane • Small applicator brush • Super glue or 2-part epoxy • Optional: bail or pin back

INSTRUCTIONS: Position 1¼" frame over transferred image, push partially in, being careful not to touch the image. Use a tissue blade to trim excess clay from each side. Push frame all the way down until flush with bottom of clay. Trim again, shave excess clay off bottom of frame. Stamp #1 Black clay, apply Gold Metallic Rub-On with sponge applicator. Set in 2" frame according to instructions above. Trim #5 Black clay to size slightly larger than 2" frame. Turn framed piece over, place the thin clay sheet over back of frame. Cover with non-stick paper, roll with acrylic brayer to bond the 2 pieces. Turn base over, trim excess clay with tissue blade. Apply a thin line of TLS around back edge of the top piece. Place top piece on base, press firmly. Bake according to manufacturer's directions. When cool, remove frames. Apply Flecto Varathane to base, let dry completely. Glue frames to clay using super glue or epoxy. Glue on pin back if desired.

Beautiful pins and pendants to wear and to share.

Olga Pendant

MATERIALS: Image, Olga
• Black clay • *All Night Media* Leaf Pattern Rubber Stamp
• Bail • Silver and Nubian Metallic Rub-Ons
INSTRUCTIONS: See instructions on page 8 for Geisha pin.

TIP
Experiment with different colors of background clay and rub-ons to achieve a number of metallic effects.

Dream Song Pin

MATERIALS: Image, Dreaming
• Texture from handmade mold • Black clay • Bail or pin back • Copper Metallic Rub-On
INSTRUCTIONS: See instructions on page 8 for Geisha pin.

Framed Tassel Pendants

with Mini-Masterpieces

Victorian Lady with Bird Necklace

MATERIALS: Basic Tool Kit • Image, Birds at Breakfast transferred onto #1 White clay (See pages 4-5) • Gold clay • Translucent *Liquid Sculpey* (TLS) • 2" Round brass frame • Eye pins, three ½" and two 2" or 2½" • Approximately 24" of brass mesh for necklace • 4 Brass end caps • 6 Jump rings • Necklace clasp • Beads • Tassel • Round-nose pliers • Chain-nose pliers • Flush cutter • Craft knife • 2-Part epoxy

INSTRUCTIONS:

Drill 3 holes for eye pins. Position 2" round frame over transferred image, making sure the holes are where you want them. Push frame partially into clay, use craft knife to trim off excess clay. Push frame down until flush with bottom of clay. Trim again, remove any remaining clay on frame. Roll out Gold clay on #5 setting. Apply TLS around the edge of back of framed piece. Place framed piece on Gold clay, press firmly. Trim around entire frame with a craft knife. Insert ½" eye pins in the 3 holes, being careful not to pierce the clay on either side. Bake according to clay manufacturer's directions. Cool, partially remove eye pins, apply super glue or epoxy. Immediately reinsert pins flush with frame. Let glue set. Arrange selected beads on a long eye pin. Form a loop at 1 end. Cut 2 pieces of brass mesh to desired length. Use epoxy to attach brass end caps. Allow glue to set. Attach jump rings and clasp to one end of each piece. Join 1 end of a beaded eye pin to 1 end cap with a jump ring, repeat on other side. Join other end of the beaded eye pin to the eye pin on framed piece with a jump ring. Repeat on other side. Attach a tassel to bottom jump ring.

Santa Necklace

This is one of innumerable variations of the 'Lady with Bird' necklace. Choose any picture with a composition suited to a round frame.

> TIP: For a more finished look, stamp or texture the Gold clay that is backing the framed piece.

1. Push frame partially into the clay, trim edges. Repeat until the frame is flush with your work surface.

2. Apply glue to partially removed eye pins, then push eye pins completely in.

Brass Frames Sizes

2" Square
Brass Frame

1$\frac{3}{4}$" Round
Brass Frame

1$\frac{1}{2}$" Square
Brass Frame

2" Round
Brass Frame

1$\frac{1}{4}$" Square
Brass Frame

Drilling Template
Drill 3 holes for eye pins.
for Lady and Santa Pendants

1" Square
Brass Frame

TIP: Place round brass frame into a sturdy clamp. This will keep the frame stable for easier drilling.

3. Arrange beads on an eye pin, form a loop at the end.

4. Glue end caps to brass mesh.

Our little girl medallion works as a focal point in a beautiful necklace as well as a box ornament.

And, check out the fabulous wooden box with framed kittens!

Little Girl with Grapes Necklace
Image, Girl with Grapes
This is another variation of the 'Lady with Bird' necklace - page 10.
TIP: The Red beads in this project are vintage 1950's. Look for vintage beads in thrift shops and antique stores to give your necklace a unique look. If you use larger beads, they may need to be strung on longer eye pins.

Girl with Grapes Box
MATERIALS: Basic Tool Kit • Image, Girl with Grapes transferred onto #1 White clay (See pages 4-5) • Gold clay • Translucent *Liquid Sculpey* (TLS) • *Rubber Stampede* grapes rubber stamp • 2" Round brass frame • Small paper mache box • *Plaid* Folk Art Poetry Green acrylic paint • Disposable brush • Sponge wedge • Inks, Sepia and Metallic Gold • 4 Beads for feet
INSTRUCTIONS:
Paint box with 2 coats of Poetry Green. Sponge on Sepia ink to antique the box. Randomly stamp Metallic Gold grape image onto box. Position 2" round frame over transferred image. Push frame partially into clay, use a sharp craft knife to trim off excess clay. Push frame all the way down until flush with bottom of clay. Trim again, remove any remaining clay on frame. Roll out Gold clay on #5 setting. Apply TLS around edge of the back of framed piece. Place framed piece on the Gold clay, press firmly. Trim around entire frame with craft knife. Bake according to clay manufacturer's directions. After baking, remove and clean the frame. Super glue it onto the clay image. Glue the beads on for feet.

Pins, Pendants and Boxes too!

with Mini-Masterpieces

Cat Lover's Wooden Box

MATERIALS: Basic Tool Kit • Images, Kitten in the Mirror and 2 cat quotes transferred onto #1 White clay (See pages 4-5) • Gold clay • Translucent *Liquid Sculpey* (TLS) • 2" and two 1½" square brass frames • Unfinished wooden box • 4 wooden balls for feet • Small round wooden piece • Metal charm for knob • Gesso • Disposable foam brushes • Sponge wedges • Sandpaper • Delta Ceramcoat Old Parchment acrylic paint • *Delta* Ceramcoat Gleams Metallic Bronze acrylic paint • *Golden Glazes* (Rust, Burnt Umber, Yellow Ochre) • Super glue • E6000 glue • Tacky glue

INSTRUCTIONS:
Sand an unfinished wooden box, apply a coat of gesso. Let dry. Sand and wipe clean. Paint inside of box with Metallic Bronze.

Paint outside with 2 coats of Old Parchment. Sponge on glazes. Paint the feet with Metallic Bronze, glue to box with E6000. Position 2" square frame over the transferred image. Push the frame partially into clay, use a sharp craft knife to trim off excess clay. Push frame all the way down until flush with bottom of clay. Trim again, remove any remaining clay on the frame.

Roll out Gold clay on #5 setting. Apply TLS around edge of the back of framed piece. Place framed piece on the Gold clay, press firmly. Trim around entire frame with craft knife. Repeat with the 2 smaller frames. Bake according to clay manufacturer's directions. Cool completely. Remove and clean frames. Super glue them back onto the clay images. Glue framed images to box top with tacky glue. Make a knob by painting a small wooden piece with Metallic Bronze. Glue charm to the wooden piece, glue finished piece to the front of the lid.

Pamphlet-Style Text Pages

INSTRUCTIONS: Cut a piece of heavy decorative paper twice the width of one cover and just slightly smaller than the height. If paper is printed on 1 side only, glue a strip down the middle of unprinted side so pattern will show through the spine to outside. Fold in half, crease with bone folder. Cut text paper or cardstock the same size as decorative paper. Fold each sheet in half, crease with bone folder. Nest pages and clip together, trim so edges are even. Nest text pages inside decorative paper. Use needle tool or awl to make 4 holes in the nested pages, 3 evenly spaced and 1 about ⅛" above top hole. Begin sewing from the outside at 2nd hole from the top. Leave a tail the length of the book. Sew in and out of holes to the bottom, then up through top hole. Leave another tail on outside, knot the 2 tails together. Apply a thin layer of glue to inside of back cover, leaving a ½" strip next to book spine. Lay back cover paper on the cover with the fold extending just slightly beyond the edge of the cover, fold toward inside of book. Smooth the paper in place, remove any excess glue. Apply super glue to the ½" strip, smooth the paper until glue has set. Repeat with front cover. Open book flat, paper side down, let dry completely. Cut a bundle of coordinating fibers twice the height of book. Tie securely in the middle. Add beads and charms. Use the 2 thread tails to attach fiber bundle to book.

Binding the Pages

Nest folded text pages inside decorative paper. Make 4 holes with a needle tool.

Sew text papers pamphlet-style, leaving 2 thread tails on the outside, knot together.

1. Insert the framed piece into the cover from underneath.

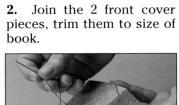

2. Join the 2 front cover pieces, trim them to size of book.

3. Join the 2 back cover pieces. Trim, apply Copper Metallic Rub-On.

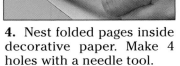

4. Nest folded pages inside decorative paper. Make 4 holes with a needle tool.

5. Sew pamphlet-style, leaving 2 thread tails on the outside, knot together.

6. Glue the decorative paper to covers. Open the book flat to dry.

7. Make a fiber bundle to embellish the book.

With a flavor from the orient this wonderful little book shines with a metallic copper sheen.

What better place to record your thoughts and memories.

Back of Book

Beautiful Book Covers

Geisha Book

MATERIALS: Basic Tool Kit • Image, Utamaro's Geisha transferred onto #1 White clay (See pages 4-5) • Burnt Umber clay • *Hero Arts* Chinese Newspaper WordPrint rubber stamp • 1¼" Square brass frame • Decorative paper • Text paper • Copper Metallic Rub-On • Sponge applicator • *Flecto* Varathane • Small brush • Needle tool • Tapestry needle • Waxed thread • Fibers • Charms and beads • Craft knife • Acrylic brayer • Super glue • Sobo or tacky glue

INSTRUCTIONS:
Position 1¼" frame over transferred image, push partially into clay, being careful not to touch image. Use a tissue blade to trim excess clay from each side. Push frame all the way down until flush with bottom of clay, trim again. Roll out 2 pieces of #1 Burnt Umber clay, stamp each piece. Impress the outline of an empty frame in center of 1 cover. Cut the center square out with craft knife. Smooth cut edges, insert the framed piece of clay from underneath the cover. Roll a piece of #5 Burnt Umber clay slightly larger than the cover. Lay #1 piece on top of the #5 piece, trim them together. Use an eye make up sponge to apply copper Metallic Rub-On to top and sides. Roll a piece of #5 Burnt Umber slightly larger than back cover. Turn cover face down, apply backing piece with an acrylic brayer. Turn piece face up, trim. Apply Copper Metallic Rub-On. Bake both covers according to the clay manufacturer's instructions. If necessary, cover and weight pieces down as they are cooling. When completely cooled, apply a coat of Flecto Varathane or other finish formulated especially for polymer clay. Nest folded text pages inside decorative paper and sew. Glue the decorative paper to inside covers. Open the book flat to dry. Embellish book with fibers, beads and charms.

continued from pages 14 - 15

Umbrella Sisters Art Book

MATERIALS: Basic Tool Kit • Image, Umbrella Ladies transferred onto #1 White clay (See pages 4-5) • Burnt Umber clay • Rubber Stamps (*Sonlight Crafts* oval frame; *Limited Edition* 'ART') • Text paper • Deep Gold Metallic Rub-On • Sponge applicator • *Flecto* Varathane • Small brush • Craft knife • Acrylic brayer • Waxed paper • Seed beads • Sobo or tacky glue

INSTRUCTIONS: Follow the basic instructions for the Geisha Book on page 15.

TIP: A large or irregularly shaped image can be framed with seed beads instead of a metal frame. After making the cover cut-out for the image, trace the outline of opening on a piece of waxed paper. Cut out the paper shape and use it as a pattern for cutting out the image. When cover is assembled, press a string of seed beads into clay around image and bake.

Stamp 'Art' on Back Cover

Beautiful Book Covers

It never ceases to amaze me what can now be done with rubber stamps and clay.

The clay here has been stamped, had images transferred to it and then pages added inside to create these lovely books.

Santa Accordion Book

MATERIALS: Basic Tool Kit • Image, Santa with Children transferred onto #1 White clay (See pages 4-5) • Black clay • *JudiKins* Christmas frame rubber stamp • 2" square brass frame • Text paper • Silver Metallic Rub-On • Sponge applicator • *Flecto* Varathane • Small brush • Craft knife • Acrylic brayer • 3/8" ribbon (length will vary according to thickness of pages) • Sobo or tacky glue • Charm for back cover (optional)

INSTRUCTIONS: Follow the basic instructions for the Geisha Book on page 15.

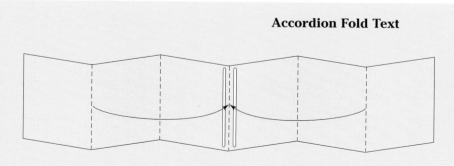

Accordion Fold Text

Cut the text paper the height of the book, fold accordion-style. Add glue to spine as shown and press together. Let dry.

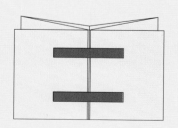

Cut 2 pieces of ribbon, glue to the spine to secure pages.

1. After baking, apply Gold paint marker to the edges.

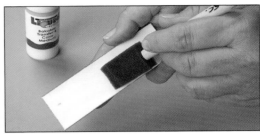

2. Brush TLS onto the back of the baked transferred image.

3. Press image into the plain side of textured clay.

4. Trim, punch a hole for the tassel.

Girl in Red Bookmark

MATERIALS: Basic Tool Kit • Image, Girl with Grapes transferred onto #5 White clay (See pages 4-5) • Red clay • Translucent *Liquid Sculpey* (TLS) • Disposable foam brush • Gold paint marker • Gold tassel with cord

INSTRUCTIONS:

Trim and bake image. Apply Gold metallic marker to edges. Make a textured sheet of #5 Red clay slightly larger than image. Turn it textured side down. Apply a thin layer of TLS to back of baked image. Press transferred image firmly into the Red clay. Trim, leaving a border of colored clay. Use a small straw to make a hole at the top of the bookmark. Bake according to clay manufacturer's directions. Cool slightly, weight with flat object such as a smooth ceramic tile, if necessary. Add a tassel.

Butterfly Gallery Bookmark

MATERIALS: Image, Butterflies • Textured Blue clay • Translucent *Liquid Sculpey* (TLS) • Disposable foam brush • Gold paint marker • Blue cord

INSTRUCTIONS: Follow instructions for Girl in Red bookmark to complete the project.

Geisha Bookmark

MATERIALS: Image, Utamaro's Geisha • Textured Gold clay • Translucent *Liquid Sculpey* (TLS) • Disposable foam brush • Gold paint marker • Fibers

INSTRUCTIONS: Follow the instructions for the Girl in Red bookmark to complete the project.

Terrific Bookmarks

Bookmark lovers, these terrific page markers are just what you need to add to your collection! With little time and effort, you can make these mini-masterpieces to keep or give as gifts. They are perfect alone or slipped inside a book as a second gift. Bookmarks also make great embellishments on gift wrap.

You will enjoy all the different looks you are able to achieve by using different stamps and image transfers.

Pendants . . . Elegance and Flair

with Leather Cord and Mini-Masterpieces

This simple but elegant piece is all that's needed to make that plain outfit shine. The brass frame holds the Asian image secure. The closure, eye pin and bail are also made of brass.

Although the pendant appears heavy it is really feather light and of course the black leather cord is not only light, it goes with everything.

TIP: Place the round brass frame into a sturdy clamp. This will keep the frame stable for easier drilling.

Drill a hole in the frame large enough to accommodate an eye pin. Position the frame over the image, with the drilled hole at the top.

1. Place the framed piece on the backing clay and trim.

2. Glue end caps onto cords.

Round Geisha Pendant with Leather Cord

MATERIALS: Basic Tool Kit • Image, Geisha Head transferred onto #1 White clay (See pages 4-5) • Gold clay • Translucent *Liquid Sculpey* (TLS) • 1¾" Round brass frame • Black leather cord • Brass end caps • Brass bail • ½" Eye pin • Jump rings • Lobster clasp • Chain-nose pliers • Craft knife • Super glue or 2-part epoxy • E6000 glue
INSTRUCTIONS:
Drill a hole in frame large enough to accommodate the eye pin. Position frame over transferred image, with the hole at the top. Push frame partially into clay. Use a craft knife to trim off excess clay. Push frame all the way down until flush with bottom of clay. Trim again, remove any remaining clay on frame. Roll out #5 Gold clay. Texture it, if desired. Apply TLS around the edge of back of framed piece. Place it on the Gold clay, press firmly. Trim around entire piece with craft knife. Insert eye pin into the clay. Bake according to clay manufacturer's directions. When cool, partially remove eye pin and apply super glue or epoxy. Immediately re-insert eye pin flush with the frame. Determine how many strands of cord the necklace will have, select end caps large enough to hold your selection snugly. Cut strands to desired length. Use E6000 to glue one set of cord ends into an end cap. If the end cap fits through the bail, repeat on other end. If not, do this as the final step. Slide bail onto the cords. Connect bail to eye pin with a jump ring. Attach jump rings and lobster clasp to end caps.

Create Fabulous
Necklaces with Elegant
Pendants!

𝒫endants . . .

with Leather Cord

continued from pages 20 - 21

TIP: Attach end caps to the cords and add clasps.

TIP: Instead of an eye pin to attach pendant to bail, 18 gauge wire can be used. Drill holes in frame approximately ½" apart. Form a half circle out of 18 gauge wire. Insert wire into the holes before baking. After baking, remove wire. Add bail before gluing wire into place.

TIP: Instead of framing your pendant, use a craft knife or shape cutter. After baking, apply metallic Gold or Silver to edges with a paint marker.

Square Geisha Pendant
MATERIALS: Basic Tool Kit • Image, Utamaro's Geisha transferred onto #1 White clay (See pages 4-5) • Gold clay • Translucent *Liquid Sculpey* (TLS) • 1¼" square brass frame • Tan leather cord • Brass end caps • Brass bail • 18 gauge wire • Jump rings • Lobster clasp • Wire cutters • Chain-nose pliers • Craft knife • Super glue or 2-part epoxy • E6000 glue
INSTRUCTIONS: Follow the basic instructions for the Round Geisha Book Pendant on page 20.

Butterfly Pendant With Charm
MATERIALS: Basic Tool Kit • Image, Butterflies transferred onto #1 White clay (See pages 4-5) • Red clay • Square cutter • Rust and Natural colored leather cord • Brass end caps • Brass bail • Jump rings • Lobster clasp • Chain-nose pliers • Craft knife • Super glue or 2-part epoxy • E6000 glue • Eye pin • Butterfly and several small beads
INSTRUCTIONS: Follow the basic instructions for the Round Geisha Book Pendant on page 20.

Venice Skyline Pendant
MATERIALS: Basic Tool Kit • Image, Venice Engraving transferred onto #1 White clay (See pages 4-5) • Black clay • Square cutter • Silver necklace cable • Silver bail • Jump ring • Eye pin • Chain nose pliers • Craft knife • Super glue or 2-part epoxy
INSTRUCTIONS: Follow the basic instructions for the Round Geisha Book Pendant on page 20.

Fabulous Necklace Pendants with Elegance and Flair!

Madonna

Madonna and Child

Umbrella Ladies

Venice Engraving

COPY PERMISSION - You may copy or photocopy patterns in this book for personal use or to make items to sell for 'pin money'. You do not have permission to sell the patterns. When you employ help making items or make more than 12 to sell, you have exceeded this permission.

These images have been reversed and are ready to be copied onto Lazertran Silk image transfer paper.

Geisha with Mirror

Cat with Cello

Girl with Flowers

Woman with Sombrero

Geisha with Cat

Umbrella Ladies

Rosy-Cheeked Girl

Curly-Haired Girl

These images have been reversed and are ready to be copied onto Lazertran Silk image transfer paper.

Utamaro Geisha

Butterflies

Chinese Bird

These images have been reversed and are ready to be copied onto Lazertran Silk image transfer paper.

Cowgirl

Girl with Grapes

Santa with Children

Geisha Head

Japanese Woodcut

COPY PERMISSION - You may copy or photocopy patterns in this book for personal use or to make items to sell for 'pin money'. You do not have permission to sell the patterns. When you employ help making items or make more than 12 to sell, you have exceeded this permission.

These images have been reversed and are ready to be copied onto Lazertran Silk image transfer paper.

Chrysanthemum Girl #1

Chrysanthemum Girl #2

Olga

Chrysanthemum Girl #3

Dreaming

Birds at Breakfast

Lady in Hat

These images have been reversed and are ready to be copied onto Lazertran Silk image transfer paper.

Kittens in a Bowl

Kitten in the Mirror

"The smallest feline is a
masterpiece." DaVinci

Time spent with cats is
never wasted." Colette

"The fog comes on little cat
feet." Sandburg

"There are no ordinary
cats." Colette

French Script

Italian Script

Child with Cat

These images have been reversed and are ready to be copied onto Lazertran Silk image transfer paper.

Clay Masterpieces
from Flea Market Finds

Turn inexpensive jewelry, belt buckles and found objects from flea markets and thrift shops into tiny masterpieces. They can be funky or elegant, sweet or nostalgic, depending on the choice of images and embellishments.

An Assortment of Possibilities

Rectangle: Repaint an old belt buckle, add letter charms and it becomes a unique pin or pendant.

Mother of Pearl Ovals: Turn a beautiful mother of pearl belt buckle into an elegant brooch. The addition of a charm with a colored stone adds just the right finishing touch. Add glass accent beads to give a vintage belt buckle new life.

Green Circle: Replace some of the beads on an old earring with brass stars and turn it into a festive Christmas pin.

Square Brass Piece: Use part of a giant earring as a background for a framed image. Add interest with a word charm and scrap wire.

Large Open Circle: Send a message with a pin made from part of a discarded earring.

Brass Heart: Combine little bits and pieces of broken jewelry to make a sweet heart pin.

Clay Masterpieces from Flea Market Finds

MATERIALS: Basic Tool Kit • Images transferred onto #3 White clay (See pages 4-5) • Charms and beads • Seed beads • Flush cutters and/or wire cutters • Sandpaper • Craft knife • Super glue or 2-part epoxy • E6000 glue • Tacky glue

INSTRUCTIONS:

To prepare the piece, remove pin backs, belt hooks and other findings that are not needed. Smooth sharp edges with sandpaper. Use paint or faux patina to cover worn or ugly surfaces. Some old copper and brass pieces have developed an antique patina that you may want to leave as is. Drill holes, as necessary, for hanging beads and charms. Position frame over transferred clay, press it hard enough to leave an outline. Cut about ⅛" inside outline with craft knife. Check fit, trim with craft knife, as necessary. Bake following manufacturer's directions. Glue frame onto image with super glue or epoxy. (If back of frame has a definite recessed area, make a pattern of that, use it to cut out the image.) To finish your piece, glue a string of seed beads around exposed edges of clay with tacky glue. Add embellishments, glue on pin back or bail with super glue or epoxy,

Turn a new frame into old with a faux pati-
a and some tiny charms.

Some pieces are too heavy to wear as pins.
Vintage belt buckles make great frames to display on tiny easels or hang from ribbons.

Glue a row of seed beads around the back edge
of the clay piece to give your projects a more finished look.

Fabulous Octagonal Display Box

with Mini-Masterpiece

The mystery of the orient is alive and well in this fabulous display box. Create beautiful clay panels with asian images to adorn the sides. Add the finishing touch by attaching a tassel to each corner of the octagonal box.

Add a Handle to tTop

Add Tassels to Sides

Add Feet to Bottom

Hexagonal Geisha Box with Tassels

MATERIALS: Basic Tool Kit • Image, Japanese Woodcut transferred onto #3 White clay (See pages 4-5) • Large hexagonal paper mache box • *Delta* Ceramcoat Red Iron Oxide acrylic paint • Disposable brush • Needle tool • Chain-nose pliers • Sponge wedge • Walnut ink • 7 Carved cinnabar beads, 6 for feet, 1 for top • Black stone donut • Small flat charm • Small Black beads • 6 Black tassels • Jump rings • Gold paint marker • E6000 glue • Tacky glue

INSTRUCTIONS:

Use needle tool to make a small hole at each corner of box lid. Paint box and lid with 2 coats of Red Iron Oxide. Let dry completely. Paint inside of box or line it with decorative paper for a more finished look. Sponge on Walnut ink to create an antique effect. Glue bead feet on with E6000. Trim transferred image with rounded corners. Bake according to manufacturer's directions. Apply Gold paint marker to edges. Glue image onto box with tacky glue. Make a string of Black beads long enough to go around the image. Apply thin line of tacky glue around image. Lay string of beads evenly around edge. Remove some beads, if necessary, to make a perfect fit, cut off thread ends. Attach jump ring to each corner of lid. Pull each tassel as far through jump ring as possible, then pull head of tassel through loop to attach it to jump ring. Glue a small charm over 1 hole of the cinnabar bead. Glue stone donut to center of lid and the bead into center of donut.

1. Make a small hole at each corner of the lid for tassels. Paint box and lid.

2. After painting the box and lid with 2 coats of paint, use a sponge to apply Walnut ink.

3. Glue one cinnabar bead to each corner of the box bottom.

4. Apply Gold paint marker to edges of the baked image.

5. Glue the image to one side of box, add a frame of seed beads.

6. Attach tassels to jump rings on the lid.

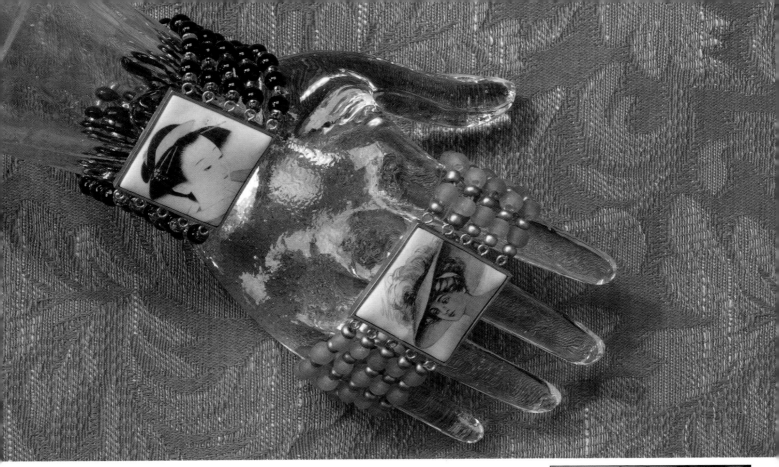

𝓑eaded 𝓑racelets

with Mini-Masterpieces

The effortless beauty of form and style are not wasted on these fashion beauties. Wear yours with style.

Geisha Five Strand Stretch Bracelet

MATERIALS: Basic Tool Kit • Image, Geisha Head transferred onto #1 White clay (See pages 4-5) • Gold clay • Translucent *Liquid Sculpey* (TLS) • 1¼" Square brass frame • Ten ½" eye pins • Stretch Magic bead cord • Small alligator clips • Contrasting beads • 527 Glue • 2-Part epoxy

INSTRUCTIONS:

Drill 5 holes on opposite sides of 1¼" frame. Position frame over image, push partially in, being careful not to touch image. Use tissue blade to trim excess clay from each side. Push frame all the way down until it is flush with bottom of clay. Trim again, shave excess clay off bottom of frame. Roll out Gold clay on #5 setting. Apply TLS around edge of the back of framed piece. Place framed piece on the Gold clay, press firmly. Trim off excess clay. Insert ½" eye pins in holes, being careful not to pierce the clay on either side. Bake according to manufacturer's directions. Cool, partially remove eye pins. Apply epoxy, push the pins completely into frame. Let dry. Subtract 1¼" from wrist measurement. Cut 5 lengths of Stretch Magic at least twice as long as this measurement. Thread one length through a large-holed bead first, then two more beads, through the loop of one eye pin, then back through the beads. Tie a square knot, pull tight so knot is inside bead. Apply a dot of glue, let dry. Repeat with remaining four strands. String beads to desired length, then attach strands to the other side of the frame.

Lady in Big Hat Bracelet

Image, Lady in Hat transferred onto #1 White clay (See pages 4-5).

INSTRUCTIONS: To make this bracelet or any variation of the Geisha Five Strand bracelet, follow instructions above.

1. Bake the framed image, glue eye pins in place.

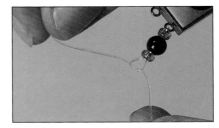

2. Thread a length of elastic bead cord through 3 beads, an eye pin and back through the beads. Knot and glue before trimming cord.

3. Attach the strand of beads to other side in the same manner.

Kitten in the Mirror Bracelet

MATERIALS: Basic Tool Kit • Image, Kitten in the Mirror transferred onto #1 White clay (See pages 4-5) • Gold clay • Translucent *Liquid Sculpey* (TLS) • 1" Square brass frame • Six ½" Eye pins • *Stretch Magic* bead cord • Small alligator clips • 3 Types of beads for braided strands • 6 Beads with large holes • 2-Part epoxy • 527 Glue
INSTRUCTIONS:

Drill 3 holes on opposite sides of 1" frame. Position frame over transferred image, push partially in, being careful not to touch image. Use a tissue blade to trim excess clay off each side. Push frame all the way down until it is flush with the bottom of the clay. Trim again, shave excess clay from bottom of frame. Roll out Gold clay on #5 setting. Apply TLS around edge of the back of framed piece. Place framed piece on Gold clay, press firmly. Trim off excess clay. Insert ½" eye pins in the holes, being careful not to pierce clay on either side. Bake according to manufacturer's directions. Cool, remove eye pins. Subtract 1" from wrist measurement. Cut 9 lengths of Stretch Magic at least twice as long as this measurement. Thread 3 lengths through a large holed bead, through loop of an eye pin, then back through the bead. Tie a square knot, pull tight so knot is inside the bead. Apply a dot of glue. Add several more beads to strand, cut off remaining short end of Stretch Magic. Continue adding beads until strand is desired length. Repeat with the other 2 strands. Push each strand until it fits snugly against the large bead. Secure ends with alligator clips. Braid the 3 strands loosely, secure with an alligator clip. Check fit, add or subtract

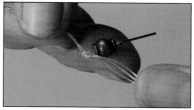

1. Bake framed image, remove eye pins. **2.** Thread 3 lengths of elastic bead cord through a large-holed bead, an eye pin, and back through the bead. Knot, glue before trimming.

3. Bead each strand to desired length, braid strands loosely. **4.** Glue eye pins on each end of braided pieces into the frame.

beads, as needed. Knot strands together, apply a dot of glue. Run strands through a large bead, an eye pin, then back through the bead. Knot, pull tight so knot is inside the bead, apply a dot of glue. Let dry, clip off the tails. Make 2 more sets of braided beads. Insert eye pins partially into the frame. Apply epoxy, push pins completely in. Let dry.

Woman with Sombrero Bracelet

Image, Woman with Sombrero transferred onto #1 clay (See pages 4-5)
INSTRUCTIONS:

Follow instructions for Kitten in the Mirror Bracelet. Choose beads that complement the image.

Clever Booklace Pendants

with Mini-Masterpieces

What clever little pendants these are! The frame of the pendant holds its own secret accordion booklet

The cover of the booklet is a clay transfer and the back cover is stamped in a design, then finished with metallic Rub-On.

1. Trim stamped clay for the back cover.

2. Apply metallic Gold to inside edges of the covers.

3. Glue end pages of the mini accordion booklet text to the inside of covers.

4. Attach beaded eye pin to the loop at the top of the frame.

5. Attach beads and charms to frame with thread.

Each little frame opens from the top to reveal the mini-booklet inside.

TIP: Press a charm into the back cover clay before baking. When cool, remove the charm and glue in place.

TIP: Choose a rubber stamp design for the back of your pendant.

Open booklet to reveal messages, images and photos inside.

Various stamps can be used to create the clay backs of the pendants.

Geisha with Mirror Booklace

MATERIALS FOR BOOK: Basic Tool Kit • Image, Geisha with Mirror transferred onto #3 White clay (See pages 4-5) • Black clay • *Hero Arts* Chinese Newspaper WordPrint rubber stamp • Book cover template • Gold Metallic Rub-On • Metallic Gold paint marker • Paper images to decorate book pages • Text paper • Stamps, inks and pens • Paper cutter • Sobo or tacky glue

INSTRUCTIONS:

Use book cover template to make a pattern from cardboard or heavy paper. Stamp #3 Black clay, use pattern as a guide for trimming the clay. Apply Gold Metallic Rub-On to top and sides with sponge applicator. Trim transferred image piece, bake both according to clay manufacturer's directions. Use paint marker to apply Metallic Gold to the White edges of image piece and edges of the back side. Cut a piece of text paper approximately 1½" wide. The length will depend on the thickness of the paper and type of embellishment to be used inside. Fold the paper accordion style, stamp, emboss, write or draw on it as desired. Glue the end pages to inside of front and back covers.

MATERIALS FOR EMBELLISHED FRAME: Antique Gold hinged brass frame • Eye pin • Assorted beads • 'Dream' charm • Beading needle and thread • Leather, satin or rubber cord • Wire cutters • Chain-nose and round-nose pliers • Jewelry glue or clear nail polish

Follow instructions below.

```
Book Cover
Template
```

INSTRUCTIONS: Drill 2 holes in bottom of frame spaced the same as holes in the charm. To add beads and the word charm to bottom of frame, run a threaded needle through one hole from the inside of the frame. Leave a tail on inside. Run needle through a small bead and 1 jump ring of the word charm, then back through bead to the inside of the frame. Continue to 2nd hole, repeat, leaving another tail. Double knot the tails, apply jewelry glue or polish. Let dry, trim ends of thread.

Add beads to eye pin, leaving enough wire to form a loop to accommodate thickness of the cord on which booklace will hang. Open eye pin, attach it to loop at top of the hinged frame.

continued from pages 36 - 37

Musical Cat Booklace

MATERIALS: Image, Cat with Cello transferred onto #3 White clay (See pages 4-5)
• Black clay • *JudiKins* Swirls rubber stamp
• Hinged raw brass frame painted with Copper metallic acrylic paint • Gold and Blue Metallic Rub-Ons • 'Art' charm
INSTRUCTIONS: See pages 36 and 37.

Girl with Flowers Booklace

MATERIALS: Image, Girl with Flowers transferred onto #3 White clay (See pages 4-5)
• Burnt Umber clay • Hinged raw brass frame with faux patina • *All Night Media* Leaf pattern rubber stamp • Copper and Blue Metallic Rub-Ons • Purse or envelope charm
• Assorted beads • Eye pins
INSTRUCTIONS: See pages 36 and 37.

TIP: Use a paint pen or marker to color the word charm to coordinate with the frame.

TIP: For a different look, paint raw brass frame with acrylic paints or apply a faux patina. Use a sponge applicator to apply the paint and follow manufacturer's directions.

Each little frame opens from the top to reveal the mini-booklet inside.

Fronts and backs of booklets

Clever Booklace Pendants

More clever booklace pendants to make and fire your imagination! Notice how each pendant takes on a look all its own when the image and finish are changed.

These pendants will be a hit.

Umbrella Sisters Booklace

MATERIALS: Image, Umbrella Ladies transferred onto #3 White clay (See pages 4-5) • Black clay • *All Night Media* Leaf Pattern rubber stamp • Hinged raw brass frame painted with Silver and Burnt Umber acrylic paint • Pewter and Nubian Metallic Rub-Ons • 'Create' charm

INSTRUCTIONS: Follow general instructions on pages 36 and 37.

Woman with Sombrero Booklace

MATERIALS: Image, Woman in Sombrero transferred onto #3 White clay (See pages 4-5) • Burnt umber clay • *JudiKins* swirls rubber stamp • Antique Gold hinged brass frame • Gold Metallic Rub-Ons • Gold star charm

INSTRUCTIONS: Follow general instructions on pages 36 and 37.

> **TIP:** Apply 2 or more Rub-On colors to give depth to the textured piece and help coordinate it with the rest of the booklace.
>
> **TIP:** Choose accent beads that pick up a focal color in the image.

Open each mini-accordion booklet to reveal the fun messages, images and photos inside.

Tiled Wall Hangings or Display Pieces

with Mini-Masterpieces

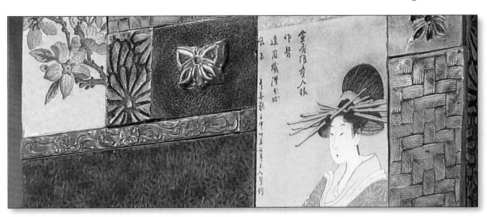

Designed to look like a heavy mosaic tile relic, this clay piece has a paper mache base which makes it very lightweight.

Follow the easy instructions to create your own work of art!

Asian Tiled Wall Hanging or Display Piece

MATERIALS: Basic Tool Kit • Images, Utamaro's Geisha and Chinese Bird transferred onto #1 White clay (See pages 4-5) • Burnt Umber clay • Rubber stamps (*JudiKins* Bollio Japan #3 and poem #2384D; *Stampa Rosa* calligraphy #J59-191 • Paper mache rectangular base • Metallic Rub-Ons • Disposable foam brush • Copper acrylic paint • Bead and coin embellishments • Sobo glue • *Flecto* Varathane

INSTRUCTIONS:

Paint all surfaces that will not be covered with clay. Trace outline of base form onto graph paper. Position, outline images and other key design elements. Draw in the placement of the textured tiles. Number each tile, identify the key tiles by name. Copy design onto cardstock. Cut out tiles to use as patterns for cutting the clay. Trim clay images to desired sizes. Texture the sheets of Burnt Umber clay. Using original design as a guide, place pattern pieces on a sheet of non-stick paper, leave space between tiles. Using paper patterns, cut out textured clay tiles. As each tile is completed, replace paper pattern with the clay tile. Make design changes now, if desired. Once layout is finalized, apply Metallic Rub-Ons to all textured tiles. Cut strips of Burnt Umber clay to fit edges of the base piece. Slice ends at an angle so corners can be mitered. Apply a thick coat of Sobo to sides of base piece. Beginning at 1 corner, press the strips of clay onto the glue all around the edge, forming a mitered seam at each corner. Apply Metallic Rub-Ons. To apply tiles to face of piece, start at 1 top corner. Work down and toward the other side. First, check fit of the tile. Apply a thick coat of Sobo to base piece, place tile. As tiles are added, make sure that they fit snugly against each other. If necessary, trim some tiles to achieve a perfect fit. Continue applying glue and tiles until surface is covered. Trim corners, apply Metallic Rub-Ons to exposed tile edges. Press embellishments into clay. Leave in place during baking. Bake according to clay manufacturer's directions, cool completely in the oven. Glue on embellishments. Apply Flecto Varathane to all tiles where Metallic Rub-Ons were used.

> **TIP:** Attach a picture hanger to back of piece, display on an easel, or to hang from a cord or ribbon, cut needed holes in the clay before baking.

1. Use paper pattern pieces to cut out textured tiles.

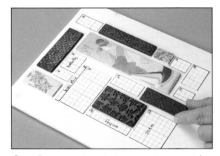

2. Lay out pattern pieces. As each clay piece is completed, place it in the design.

3. Press strips of textured clay into Sobo glue applied to the sides of base.

4. Apply Sobo and place tiles snugly against each other.

I am waiting to see...
The flowers of long ago
In my old home
Beneath the plum tree
Has the snow melted?

By Bruin
Japan ca. 1263

Just look at all the different effects you can achieve by changing the placement of your clay tiles, stamps and changing the finish of your work. You may choose to use an old photograph instead of a print. No matter what your choices, you are sure to create your own beautiful masterpiece.

Tiled Art Piece

MATERIALS: Images, Olga and Butterflies transferred onto #1 White clay (See pages 4-5) • Burnt Umber clay • Rubber stamps (*Limited Edition* DaVinci quote; *All Night Media* Leaf pattern; *JudiKins* Bollio Japan #3 • Paper Mache rectangular base

INSTRUCTIONS:

Follow general instructions for Asian Tiled Wall Hanging on page 40. Arrange tiles as desired. Display on a tabletop or hang, as desired.

Birds at Breakfast Tiled Art Piece

MATERIALS: Images, Birds at Breakfast and Venice Engraving transferred onto #1 White clay (See pages 4-5) • *Paper Inspirations* scroll rubber stamp • Black clay • Square paper mache base

INSTRUCTIONS:

Follow general instructions for Asian Tiled Wall Hanging on page 40. Arrange tiles as desired. Display on a tabletop or hang, as desired.

The text visible on the tile reads:

orte, et esu inaltra, Lo to Jerito quesat'altr
carittione de lettere la qual uolendo imparar
ffernua la regula del fottoscritto Alphabeto
a.b.c.d.ce ff g.b.i.k.l. m.n.o. p j
x.q.r.s.t.u.x.y.z &.

Tiled Wall Hangings or Display Pieces

with Mini-Masterpieces

continued from pages 40 - 41

continued from pages 40 - 41

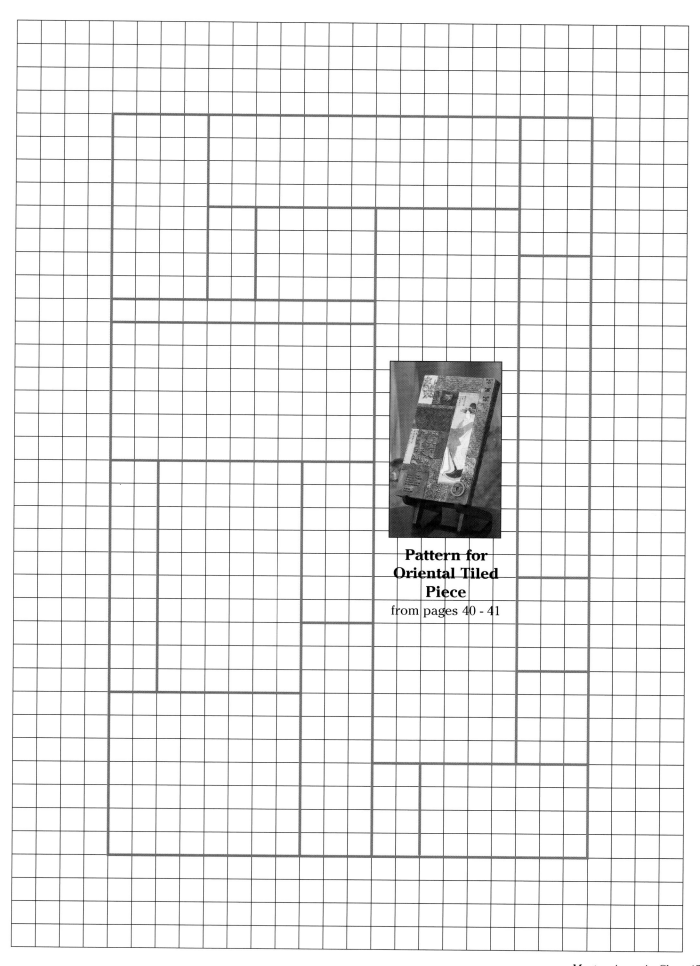

Pattern for Oriental Tiled Piece
from pages 40 - 41

Embellished Books and Journals

with Mini-Masterpieces

Add a special touch to gifts and home decor items with tiny clay embellishments. Transform books, journals, boxes, bottles and cards into unique treasures.

Transfer image to clay and then frame it to use as an embellishment.

Open and Close Jump Ring

Hold the jump ring on each side of the opening, rotate needle-nose pliers to the side opening the ring. Rotate toward opening to close.

Corrugated Cowgirl Journal

MATERIALS: Basic Tool Kit • Image, Cowgirl transferred onto #1 White clay (See pages 4-5) • Gold clay • Translucent *Liquid Sculpey* (TLS) • 2" Square brass frame • Blank journal with corrugated cardboard cover • Rusted tin • *Golden* Glazes (Burnt Umber and Cobalt Green) • Disposable foam brushes • Copper Metallic Rub-On • Matte acrylic spray sealer • Copper paint marker • Western charms • Craft knife • Super glue • E6000 glue

INSTRUCTIONS:

Brush Burnt Umber and Cobalt Green glazes on journal cover, let dry completely. Apply Copper Metallic Rub-On to top of the ridges. Spray with matte acrylic sealer. Position 2" square frame over transferred image. Push frame partially in, use a craft knife to trim off excess clay. Push frame all the way down until flush with bottom of clay. Trim again, remove any remaining clay on the frame. Roll out Gold clay on #5 setting. Apply TLS around the edge of back of framed piece. Place framed piece on the Gold clay, press firmly. Trim around entire frame with the craft knife. Bake according to clay manufacturer's directions. After baking, remove and clean frame. Super glue it back onto the clay image. Cut a square of rusted tin to fit cover. Apply Copper paint marker to edges. Punch or drill holes for jump rings, attach charms. Glue metal piece to the cover, super glue the framed image to metal piece.

Add charms and beads for dangle embellishments.

Transfer image to clay and then frame it to use as an embellishment.

Embellished Books and Boxes
with Mini-Masterpieces

Accent your room with this book box sponged with walnut ink and trimmed in gold. The Vintage Lady Treasure book is reminiscent of childhood days and secret treasures.

Or, you may want to take an existing book and wrap it in decorative paper and then add clay embellishments.

Vintage Lady Treasure Book Box

MATERIALS: Basic Tool Kit • Image, Chrysanthemum Girl transferred onto #1 White clay (See pages 4-5) • Gold clay • Translucent *Liquid Sculpey* (TLS) • 2" Square brass frame • Tiny metal frame • Paper mache book box • Decorative Gold paper • Walnut ink • Sponge wedges • Gold paint marker • Craft knife • Super glue • Tacky glue

INSTRUCTIONS:

Sponge Walnut ink onto box. Apply Gold paint marker to raised portions of the spine. Position the 2" square frame over transferred image. Push frame partially in, use a sharp craft knife to trim off excess clay. Push frame all the way down until flush with bottom of clay. Trim again, remove any remaining clay on the frame. Roll out Gold clay on #5 setting. Apply TLS around edge of the back of framed piece. Place framed piece on Gold clay, press firmly. Trim around entire frame with craft knife. Bake according to clay manufacturer's directions. After baking, remove and clean frame. Super glue it back onto the clay image. Cut a strip of Gold decorative paper, glue it to book cover. Computer generate "treasures", glue it inside the tiny metal frame. Glue framed image and tiny frame onto the Gold paper.

A Boy and His Cat Blank Book

MATERIALS:

Basic Tool Kit

• Images, Child with Cat and Cat Quote transferred onto #3 White clay (See pages 4-5) • Blank book • Decorative paper • Black ribbon • Black seed beads • Gold paint marker • Double-sided tape • Matte acrylic spray sealer • Tacky glue

INSTRUCTIONS:

Glue decorative paper to the cover of a blank book. Spray with matte acrylic sealer. Cut 2 pieces of Black ribbon. Attach them to the inside of book covers with double-sided tape. Glue decorative paper to inside covers. Trim the transferred images with rounded corners. Bake according to clay manufacturer's directions. Apply Gold paint marker to edges of the image pieces, glue them to book cover.

String 2 lengths of Black seed beads long enough to go around the images. Apply a thin line of tacky glue around one image. Lay string of beads evenly next to the image. Add or remove beads to make a perfect fit, cut off the thread ends. Repeat process with other image.

"Time spent with cats is never wasted."
Colette

Sharon V. Cipriano

Sharon is a talented mixed-media artist and jewelry designer who often incorporates polymer clay into her work. She frequently contributes to national art magazines and teaches popular paper arts and polymer clay workshops.

*Her web-based business, **Art Heaven**, showcases her designs and offers kits and components for creating wearable art. Sharon lives with her husband, Jack, in Scottsdale, Arizona, where she is active in the Arizona Polymer Clay Guild.*

Materials for many projects are available on Sharon's website, www.artheaven.net. Contact her at svc3@msn.com.

SUPPLIERS - Most craft and variety stores carry an excellent assortment of supplies. If you need something special, ask your local store to contact the following companies.
BRASS FRAMES & JEWELRY FINDINGS
   Metalliferous, 888-944-0909NY
FISKARS PAINT MARKERS
   Fiskars, 800-950-0203, Wausau, WI
FLECTO VARATHANE DIAMOND WOOD FINISH
   Available at home improvement and hardware stores
CERAMCOAT & GLEAMS METALLIC ACRYLIC PAINT
   Delta Technical Coatings, 800-423-4135, Whittier, CA
GOLDEN GLAZES
   Golden Artist Colors, 800-959-6543, New Berlin, NY
HEXAGONAL BOX
   Craf-T-Pedlars, 877-733-5277, Concord, CA
LAZERTRAN SILK TRANSFER PAPER
   Lazertran LLC USA, 800-245-7547, New Hyde Park, NY
POLYMER CLAY & LIQUID SCULPEY
   Polyform Products, 847-427-0020, Elk Grove Village, IL
PAPER MACHE ITEMS & PLAID ACRYLIC PAINT
   Plaid Enterprises, 800-842-4197, Norcross, GA
PEWTER WORD CHARMS & HINGED BRASS FRAMES
   Art Heaven, http://www.artheaven.net, Scottsdale, AZ
METALLIC RUB-ONS & DECORATING CHALKS
   Craf-T Products, 507-235-3996, Fairmont, MN
RUBBER STAMPS
   All Night Media, 678-291-8100, Norcross, GA
   Hero Arts, 800-822-4376, Emeryville, CA
   JudiKins, 310-515-1115, Gardena, ACA
   Limited Edition, 650-299-9700, San Carlos, CA
   Paper Inspirations, 406-756-9677, Kalispell, MT
   Rubber Stampede, 800-632-8386, Whittier, CA
   Sonlight Crafts International, 909-278-5656, Corona, CA
   Stampa Rosa, 800-554-5755, Santa Rosa, CA
STRETCH MAGIC BEAD AND JEWELRY CORD
   Pepperell Braiding, 800-343-8114, Pepperell, MA

Simple Bracelets and Necklaces

with Rubber Cord and Mini-Masterpieces

Here, vintage images have been transferred to clay to create wonderful charms that have been added to, of all things, rubber cord. But, it works!

Your teenagers will absolutely love this very modern jewelry. Get your kids and their friends involved. Have a sleep over jewelry party. You will difinitly be the coolest mom around!

TIP: Attach pendant to the clasp on one side. Attach a charm to the clasp on the other side. Wear the clasp in the front for a unique look.

Bracelets and Necklaces with Rubber Cord

MATERIALS: Basic Tool Kit • Images transferred onto #1 White clay (See pages 4-5) • Gold clay • Translucent *Liquid Sculpey* (TLS) • Square brass frames • ½" eye pins • 4mm Rubber cord • End caps • Jump rings • Needle nose pliers • Charms • Lobster clasp • Superglue or 2-part epoxy • E6000 glue

INSTRUCTIONS:

Drill a hole through 1 corner of frame. Position frame over transferred image, push partially in, being careful not to touch the image. Use a tissue blade to trim excess clay from each side. Push frame all the way down until flush with bottom of clay. Trim again, shave excess clay from bottom of frame. Roll out Gold clay on #5 setting. Apply TLS around edge of back of framed piece. Place framed piece on Gold clay, press firmly. Trim off excess clay. Insert a ½" eye pin into hole. Be careful not to pierce clay on either side. Bake as manufacturer's directs.

Cool, partially remove the eye pin. Apply superglue or epoxy, push the pin completely into frame. Let dry. Cut rubber cord to desired length or lengths. Glue end caps onto cord ends with E6000. Attach jump ring to framed piece, then to one end cap.

Attach a jump ring to a charm and lobster clasp, then to other end cap.

MANY THANKS to my friends for their wonderful help and ideas!
Kathy McMillan • Jennifer Laughlin • Patty Williams • Marti Wyble
Janie Ray • Barbara Worth • David & Donna Thomason